Tree Readings

13 Ogham Tree
Oracle

Carmen Reyes

Art by Carmen Reyes

Edited by Anne Jameson and Sara Skomitz

Gratitude

This book is dedicated
to Goddess, the Trees, &
my Sisters at the
Apple Branch ~ A Dianic Tradition
and most especially to
Bendis,
Fierce Huntress of the Two Spears
High Priestess of the Goddess,
A teacher & mentor
whose love
and dedication
made this work possible

And to Nepeta
beloved muse

Table of Contents

Acknowledgments

Robert Graves
divided the year into tree months in his
groundbreaking work
The White Goddess
Helena Paterson in her definitive work
The Handbook of Celtic Astrology
incorporated the tree month calendar
into the traditional zodiac
Tree essence makers
granted permission to reprint
their descriptions
Iris & Reed
brought focus & clarity
to this work

Introduction

Ogham (o-um)

is an ancient form of writing,
an Irish alphabet
better known as a tree alphabet.
Each letter of the alphabet is named for a tree and has
allusive metaphorical names called kennings or
bríatharogam (BRI-ath-ur-AWE-gum), word ogham.
Traditionally, there were many oghams and
ogham manuscripts reveal many interpretations by different authors.
Word ogham by Morainn mac Moín, Mac ind Óc, Con Culainn and a
modern scholar, O'Dubhain are included in this book.
Ogham, a secret language read from bottom to top offers a
powerful way of working with our tree allies through
divination and a monthly calendar.
Discover your tree allies with Celtic astrology and
learn the magical qualities of the trees with ogham.
Poetry will inspire you and
taking tree essences will enable
journey
work with the trees.

Find your tree

13 Tree signs
Find the tree that corresponds to your zodiac sign, your ascendant, and the
planets in your natal astrology chart
to find your personal tree allies
Read the tree chapter and look up correspondences for your trees in
Kennings, Charms & Treasures

Goddess Charms
(found in Kennings, Charms & Treasures)
Each tree is under the protection of a mythic Goddess who manifests reality with
tree qualities, charms and mystical symbolism

Tree Poems, Affirmations & Essences
Connect with your tree by reading their poem
Repeat tree affirmations to cultivate their qualities and take essences to
experience tree energy at a
deeper level

Tree Calendar
Work with tree energies throughout the year by using the calendar to
find a tree ally each month

The Goddess
of many names
reveals a magical forest where
you discover your tree allies,
their charms
and enchantments
Tree Readings are an oracle
of fortunes,
and the lore of ogham trees

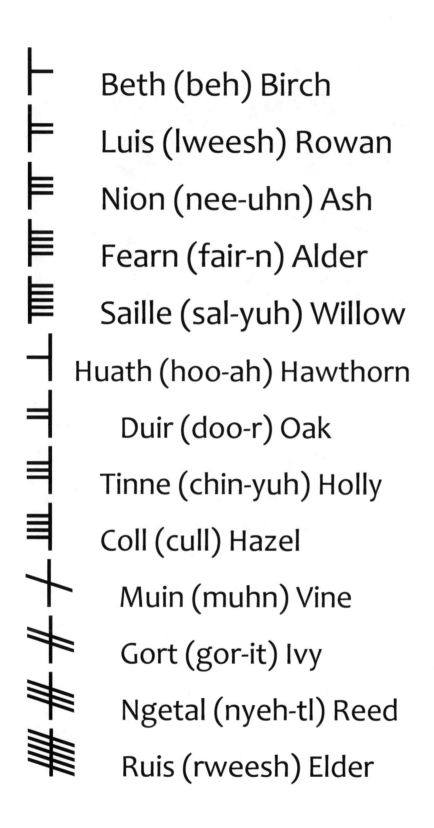

Beth (beh) Birch

Luis (lweesh) Rowan

Nion (nee-uhn) Ash

Fearn (fair-n) Alder

Saille (sal-yuh) Willow

Huath (hoo-ah) Hawthorn

Duir (doo-r) Oak

Tinne (chin-yuh) Holly

Coll (cull) Hazel

Muin (muhn) Vine

Gort (gor-it) Ivy

Ngetal (nyeh-tl) Reed

Ruis (rweesh) Elder

beautiful
fair haired Birch
shining in the starlight
you are the way shower
Lady of the Woods
Goddess Tree
transform my withered self
bring me back to life
filled with enthusiasm
to move outward
embracing the world

Birch

Beth (beh)
B

the way shower
midwife of the forest
fair hair and silvery skin
conical hat
agrimony
besom
twigs

Celtic astrology
December 22 ~ January 20
2°00` - 29°59` Capricorn

Birth, Boundaries and Purification

Birch ignites forest magic and brings new beginnings
Birch drives out the energies of the old year and offers
protection
in this moment of inception
Birch tells us to sweep away outworn attitudes and to
shape what is to come
Birch asks
"Where do we see new possibilities?"

Lady of the Woods
sweep away the old and show me the way
to new beginnings

Delight of Eye
radiant
you are
Protectress
holding all in your light
illuminate me
ancient enchantress
from the highest heights
with your beacon
of red berries

Rowan

Luis (lweesh)
L

rowan twig cross
delight of eye
quickening
red thread
vervain
flame

Celtic astrology
January 21 ~ February 17
0°00` - 27°59` Aquarius

Healing with Plants and Spirit Guides

Rowan brings inner quickening
Rowan is a bright flame that gives forewarnings of
approaching energies
Rowan reminds us to keep focus, avoid distraction,
and to look within to our spiritual strength
Rowan is a sign of protection from enchantments
Rowan indicates the power of insight
Rowan tells us to follow our inner guidance
Rowan asks
'How do we apply our insights?"

*Lady of the Mountain
with the light of the sun shine upon me
give me insight*

Fair Tree
Lady of the Woods
collector of water
beside the holy well
yours is the Key to unlock realities
woven in a lightening flash
inner and outer worlds mesh
harmoniously
in a blaze of great fire
I am swept by
wind on the waters

Ash

Nion (nee-uhn)
N

checking of peace
weaver's beam
world tree
nettle
keys

Celtic astrology
February 18 ~ March 17
28°00` Aquarius - 25°59` Pisces

Agreements and Obligations

Ash links the inner and outer worlds and weaves our
connection to our world
Ash points to the importance of our participation and our ability to support
or affect the world around us
Ash is the power of connections and of universal justice
Ash tells us to be the weaver of our fate
Ash asks
"How are we connected to the community?"

Lady of Weaving
connect me to the world around me
weave my destiny

protect us
Great Warrior Shield
hottest in the fight
with your dazzling branches
care for us
protect our hearts
shining ray of the sun
spirit guides sing sweet songs
around us
guardians
of great support

Alder

Fearn (fair-n)
F

shield of warrior bands
guardian of the heart
oracular power
containment
catkins
comfrey

Celtic astrology
March 18 ~ April 14
26°00` Pisces - 23°59` Aries

Guidance and Protection

Alder is a good council and a source of oracular powers
Alder reminds us to build bridges of lasting support, set firm foundations
for our future, and hold steadfast to what we know to be true in our heart
Alder points to emotional vulnerabilities and indicates
insight from our inner depths.
Alder brings guidance from beyond the physical realm, and the courage to
take charge of this life
Alder asks
"Where do we find shelter?"

Lady of the Water Banks
with your great shield
set firm my foundation

beautiful Lady who Weeps
by the Waters Edge
on a dream
send me the gift of eloquence
to flow
with you
whispering one
your silvery hair
swirls about me
in your healing depths

Willow

Saille (sal-yuh)
S

sacred to poets
sally tree
prophesy
luna
mugwort
dreams
basket

Celtic astrology
April 15 ~ May 12
24°00` Aries - 20°59` Taurus

Ancestral Messages and Cycles

Willow connects us with the deep unconscious parts of ourselves enabling
prophetic dreams and premonitions
Willow is a sign of intuition
Willow tells us to let go of fixed ideas and flow with
a deeper understanding of the world around us
Willow tells us to use our powers of
imagination to reach our goals
Willow asks
'What are our dreams telling us?"

Lady who Weeps by the Waters Edge
give me the vision
to imagine my future

Fair among the Flowers
your red berries
calm the painful heart
shrewd navigator
black as night
sharp thorned sister
you are a formidable impasse
I am still
in your presence

Hawthorn

Huath

H

cloutie tree
wishing well
fairy tree
meadowsweet
cleanse
cauldron
hag

Celtic astrology
May 13 ~ June 9
21°00` Taurus - 17°59 Gemini

Glamours and Misfortune

Hawthorn is a guide and protector during times of
change and growth
Hawthorn overcomes obstacles with a cleansing energy that brings peace,
helping us to face fears
Hawthorn is an impassible briar, a sanctuary from all that could
disturb us
Hawthorn tells us to wait or retreat, and when it is time to
cleanse our temple
Hawthorn asks
"What are the obstacles to our successes?"

Lady Whitethorn
surround me with your presence
give me your protection

bright and shining
is your work
Stout Doorway to Enchantments
in the wood
of beautiful acorns
you radiate great calm
guardian tree
strength in times of trouble
you make a great fortress
to guard me with
perpetual fire

Oak

Duir (doo-r)
D

door of the year
sacred grove
sacred flame
invisibility
guardian
mistletoe
acorn

Celtic astrology
June 10 ~ July 7
18°00` Gemini - 14°59` Cancer

Endurance and Triumph

Oak is a door to success and a gateway to opportunity
Oak is a bold and enduring protector
The blazing power of the oak gives the strength to
overcome all challenges, and it ensures that we have everything
needed to accomplish our goals
Oak tells us to find our courage
Oak asks
"How do we use our strengths?"

Lady of the Doorway
be my strength
in times of trouble

noblest of trees
Evergreen One
you who wear the crown
rising
from the fiery flames
with blazing armor
shining red berries
your immense positive strength
sends me forward with
strength of self and a
flowering heart

Holly

Tinne (chin-yuh)
T

bears the crown
spear
woad
starling
ingot
fire

Celtic astrology
July 8 ~ August 4
15°00` Cancer - 11°59` Leo

Creativity and Mastery

Holly battles adversity
It forges protection, prosperity, and defends us on our path
Holly shines with determined resourcefulness
It is evergreen through the dark of winter with the power of the
spiritual warrior
Holly fuels our technical skill with the strength to
meet all opposition and tells us that decisive action can
change our fortune
Holly asks
"What is worth fighting for?"

Lady of the Fighting Spirit
send me forward
with strength of self

beautiful tree
Fairest One
bless me with prophetic powers
of art and wisdom
you who dwell with your nine sisters
by the well beneath the ocean
divine the unseen mysteries
Noblest of Woods
as the shell of your nut falls away
the sweetest mystery wells up from
springs of knowledge

Hazel

Coll (cull)
C
finding out things
forked twig
hazelnuts
wisdom
clover

Celtic astrology
August 5 ~ September 1
12°00` Leo - 8°59` Virgo

Divination and Inspiration

Hazel reveals truth, showing us how to
see ourselves honestly
Hazel is the source of poetic art, a sign of creative
energy expressed as beauty
Hazel invites us to drink from an ancient well and asks
"Where do we find wisdom?"

Lady of Wisdom
bring me
good fortune
and knowledge

highest of beauty
strongest of effort
Source of Inspiration
entwining towards heaven
I give myself to you
Divine Ecstasy
spiraling up
a hill of poetry

Vine
Muin (muhn)
M

path of the voice
incantation
trickery
bramble
spiral
trust

Celtic astrology
September 2 ~ September 30
9°00` Virgo - 6°59` Libra

Channeled Creativity and Ties

Vine weaves the messages of the conscious and the
unconscious mind
Vine releases prophetic powers, dissolves the boundaries of consciousness
and frees expression
Vine is divine inspiration that leads to unexpected
truths
Vine tells us to free our mind for inspired solutions
Vine asks
"Are we receiving divine messages, can we relay them?"

Lady of Visions
send me your strongest effort
inspire me
to great deeds

Sweeter
than Grasses
strongest of powers
sheer force of will
the size of a warrior
entwining embrace
a living green canopy
Spiraling
shimmering garment
to warn me and keep me
dense thicket
about me

Ivy

Gort (gor-it)
G
sweeter than grasses
house of learning
poet's crown
labyrinth
cultivation
hunger
ivy

Celtic astrology
October 1 ~ October 29
7°00` Libra - 4°59` Scorpio

Spiritual Retreat and Restoration

Ivy leads us along the labyrinthine spiral of life to
discover hidden or mysterious things
Ivy is a source of strength and support
It is a sign of endurance, which transforms the self and leads it to
self knowledge
Ivy tells us to use self control and tap our inner strength as we set out upon
the windy path of our spiritual journey
Ivy asks
"Where does our secret garden grow?"

Lady of the Labyrinth
lend me your tenacity
to overcome circumstances

piercing wound
Healing Charm
incantation
form to form
Physician's Strength
sing the poem
healer be healed
mend what was broken
Lady's Strength attend to us
restore in us
a healthy blush

Reed

Ngetal (nyeh-tl)
Ng

robe of physicians
medicinal herbs
preservation
knowledge
memory
plantain
pen

Celtic astrology
November 1 ~ November 25
5°00` Scorpio - 2°59` Sagittarius

Pathways of Life and Sympathetic Magic

Reed represents the delicate balance between this and the Otherworld
Reed emerges from the watery depths immersing
our wounds with healing waters
Reed is the healing charm that opens old wounds so that
health can be restored
Reed is the transformative power of healing, indicating
that we attend to
our health
Reed asks
"Where are our wounds"?

Lady of Healing Charms
may I be a hollow channel
for your energy

Hylde Moer
Elder Mother
Queen of the Herbs
Great Healer
with lacy white blossoms
star umbel portals
to unseen realms
O fairy tree
Old Woman of the Hedgerow
I dance
in your procession

Elder

Ruis (rweesh)
R

healing tree
Tree of the Cailleach
redness
madder
bones
fate

Celtic astrology
November 26 ~ December 23
3°00` Sagittarius - 1°59` Capricorn

Battle Frenzy and Ecstatic Trances

Elder is a guardian tree that heals with berries and leaves
Elder is the Wishing Tree
It is a symbol of good fortune and a sign of continual change, from
birth to death and
beginnings and endings
Elder shifts from one state to another, it is in a transitional state of being
and it tells us to see beyond surface appearances
Elder asks
"What has ended and what is beginning?"

Lady of the Hedgerow
transform me
show me how to maintain balance

Kennings, Charms & Treasures

Birch
Beth (beh)

Betula alba
Betulaceae (Birch Family)

Botanical Highlights

Birches get their names from the color of their bark although the young bark of the White birch is reddish brown and takes roughly ten years to turn white. Birches have many uses and varying characteristics. The twigs of the Sweet and Black birches have a wintergreen flavor when chewed and can be used as toothbrushes. Papery bark that falls to the forest floor is rot resistant and water proof and can be gathered for starting fires or for making birch baskets. Grey birch has a triangular marking called a chevron which distinguishes it from other birches.

Tree Essence

White Birch
Betula alba
Delta Gardens ~ "Tempers an overly aggressive personality. Gives an overly masculine temperament an appreciation of its female aspects. Good for adolescents struggling with identity issues."

Silver Birch
Betula pendula
Green Man Essences ~ " '*Beauty*' The ability to experience beauty and calmness. Tolerance of self and others. For those who find it difficult to express themselves."

Black or Sweet Birch
Betula lenta
Woodland Essence ~ "Gracious. Getting in touch with inner radiance."

The name of the birch comes from the IE root *bhereg* meaning "white, bright; to shine."

Word Ogham

Morainn mac Moín ~ *"faded trunk and fair hair"*
Mac ind Óc ~ *"most silvery of skin"*
O'Dubhain ~ *"will to live"*

Fair hair and silver skin, will to live, purification
A very white tree with tendril-like branches, some Birch species have a silvery sheen to their bark.

Birth, midwife of the forest, inception, will to live
Birch is the first tree of the tree calendar year and the first to grow in areas that have been de-forested. Birch has a strong will to live although its life is short; it prepares the soil for other trees and fades when the area becomes congested. Birch is used to purify the child bed and to bless the new mother and babe. Birch creates the power of inception, the sensation that something is about to begin or is beginning.

Treasures

Agrimony ~ purification
Agrimonia eupatoria. Rosaceae (Rose Family)
Magically, agrimony eliminates negative energy and purifies, enabling growth.

Besom
A traditionally constructed broom with birch twigs bound to an ash handle with willow straps.

Birch twigs
Gather fallen twigs and tie them together with red thread to make a hand broom for sweeping away old outworn attitudes or energies.

Conical hat
In past times birch bark was made into a hat for the deceased as a symbol of rebirth between lifetimes.

Twigs, boundaries, forest magic, authority
The Latin word *batuere*, "to strike," may be the origin of the word birch. Birch twigs bound together form an ancient discipline switch. Twigs used this way give rise to the term "to go a birching." In ancient Rome, birch wands were used as a symbol of authority. Birch twigs tied together were used to "beat the boundaries" of an area. Birch is said to have authority in the forest and to have a birch wand enables command over the forest trees.

The way show-er
The white bark of the birch stands out in the forest on a dark night and helps to "show the way."

Goddess Charms

Sabd
Celtic Deer Goddess, Protectress of the Woodlands, Birth giving Goddess, gentle and graceful guide to the sacred birch grove of rebirth. Sabd, Goddess of Wild Untamed Nature, of hunting and the moon (similar qualities to Greek Artemis), prances through the forest in the form of a deer, sweeps the forest floor with Her besom (broom) and stirs up the fertile earth, preparing it for new growth.

Rowan
Luis (Iweesh)

Sorbus aucuparia
Rosaceae (Rose Family)

Botanical Highlights

The rowan or mountain ash is a small tree that rarely grows beyond 30 feet.
Rowan is unrelated to the ash tree *Fraxinus*. The rowan berry is a tiny apple called
a pome. The berries are made into bird lime, a sticky substance used to catch
birds. The rowan's specific name, *aucuparia* means a fowler, one who catches
birds.

Tree Essence

European Mountain Ash
Sorbus aucuparia
Green Man Essences ~ " '*Nature*' Attunement to the energies of nature,
particularly wood and earth. Enlarges perspectives to a cosmic level, allowing
deep understanding of the universe."

The Irish word for rowan is *caorann* (KOH-run) meaning the red one.

Word Ogham

Morainn mac Moín ~ *"delight of eye"*
Mac ind Óc ~ *"friend of cattle"*

Twigs, cross & red thread, friend of cattle
Rowan twigs are hung over the barn door to protect animals from enchantments.
Small rowan twigs are crossed and woven in place with red thread to make a
charm for protection. In past times, rowan crosses were sewn into the linings of
garments to protect the wearers from enchantments.

Delight of eye, flame, berries

The red rowan berries are an important source of food for birds and they are beautiful to see, the color of flame. They are the symbol of Brighid, the Goddess of the Bright Flame.

Healing with plants, flame

According to Erynn Rowan Laurie, "*Lus* (Luis) is most likely derived from one of two different IE roots *leuk*-'to shine,' from which the meaning 'flame' is derived or *leudh*- meaning 'to grow,' which leads to the potential meaning of 'an herb.' " [1] Medicinal herbs are transformed into healing plant-medicine by the heat of the flame.

Treasures

Attunement to nature

The rowan brings knowledge of the mysteries of nature as indicated by the five pointed star on each of its berries.

Blue Vervain ~ protection

Verbena hastata. Verbenaceae (Verbena or Vervain Family)
This is an herb that protects against enchantments; it can be worn or burned as incense.

Quickening

Seeds begin to quicken within the earth during the rowan month and there is an inner quickening within ourselves, giving the rowan the name of Quicken tree.

Spirit guides

Prayers are recited or sung as herb infusions are made to invoke the blessing of beneficial spirits.

Goddess Charms

Brigantia

Rowan belongs to the Celtic Goddess Brighid who is known as the Fiery Arrow or the Bright Flame. Rowan is associated with the fire festival Brigantia or Candlemas, dedicated to Brighid, the festival of lights also known as Imbolc. Brigantia wraps red thread about twigs of rowan to make tiny crosses for our

---

1   Laurie, *Ogham: Weaving Word Wisdom*, p. 64.

protection. She places them in a satchel containing flame bright berries, tiny apples with tiny stars upon them that bring insight and inner quickening.

Ash
Nion (nee-uhn)

Fraxinus excelsior
Oleaceae (Olive Family)

Botanical Highlights

Ash is one of the last trees to put on leaves in the spring time. Only a few trees have opposite compound leaves, the ash the box elder (maple) and the buckeye. Ash "keys" are single-winged seeds that mature in the summer then fall to the forest floor.

Tree Essence

European Ash
Fraxinus excelsior
Green Man Essences ~ " '*Strength*' Harmony with your surroundings. Feeling in tune. Flexibility and security."

White Ash
Fraxinus americana
Woodland Essence ~ "Core integrity. Standing in one's truth."

Ash is derived from the Old Norse root word *Askr*, the name of the first man in the Northern Germanic Tradition. Old Irish for ash is *fuinseóg* (FWIN-shug).

Word Ogham

Morainn mac Moín ~ *"checking of peace"*
Mac ind Óc ~ *"fight of women, boast of women, contest of women"*

Checking of peace, agreements and obligations
Communication, negotiation, fulfilling obligations and connecting people is a way to check or ensure peace; these are the actions of ash. Ash makes agreements and fulfills obligations of the family and the world at large.

Fight of women, boast of women, and contest of women
Spinning, weaving and the making of fabric has predominantly been the work of women since ancient times. Women do this work singing, boasting, telling tales and striving to do the most valuable work. They chant and recite prayers for the well being of the family and community.

Treasures

Keys
The winged seed pods of the ash called "keys" metaphorically represent keys that connect the inner and outer world.

Nettle ~ weaving
Urtica dioica. Urticaceae (Nettle Family)
Besides being an important food and plant medicine, our ancestors wove nettle to make their clothing.

Weaver's beam
Ash is connected with weaving in a literal and metaphorical sense. The weaver's beam is made of ash, a resilient and durable wood.

World tree
Ash is known as the world tree, the tree that unites the Three Worlds, the heavens above us, the sea that surrounds us, and the earth beneath us.

Goddess Charms

Nine Maidens
Their breath warms the Holy Grail, a magical cauldron of initiation and rebirth which is located in the Underworld. The Nine Maiden Goddesses offer us a Holy

Grail containing the waters of life. They weave the three worlds of land, sea and sky together with their ashen beam and unlock secrets within us with ash "keys."

Alder

Fearn (fair-n)

Alnus glutinosa
Betulaceae (Birch Family)

Botanical Highlights

In springtime the alder flowers open and expand into furry catkins. The female catkins develop into cones that remain on the tree throughout the winter.

Tree Essence

 European Alder
Alnus glutinosa
Green Man Essences ~ " 'R*elease*' Reduces nervousness and anxiety. Brings clarity of mind and eases stress. Increases flow of prana/chi."

Both the Latin and the Germanic words for alder derive from the Proto-Indo European root *el*, meaning "red" or "brown." Three dyes are made from the alder: red from the bark, brown from the twigs and green from the flowers. The leaves are so sticky they can catch flies on them when spread out upon a surface. This quality gives the alder its specific name *glutinosa*.

Word Ogham

Morainn mac Moín ~ *"shield of warrior bands"*
Con Culainn ~ *"protection of the heart"*
Mac ind Óc ~ *"guarding of milk"*
O'Dubhain ~ *"protecting the head"*

Shield of warrior bands, protection, tree that bleeds

Alder is known as a battle-witch, the "hottest" in a fight because it turns red when cut even though its wood is white. Battle-witches are warriors and the protection of a warrior is a shield. Shields overlapped make an enclosure that cannot be overtaken.

Guardian of the heart, guidance and protection

Shielding can apply to the emotions and some of our most difficult battles are fought not in the field but in the home. Alder protects our heart, the seat of our emotions and offers guidance.

Containment, guarding of milk, foundation

Literally and figuratively, the idea of containment and foundation describe alder. Alder wood was used to make milk buckets, bowls and bridge foundations.

Protecting the head

Protecting the head refers to a helmet that guards physical safety, as well as shielding ones sanity. Protection is also found in the ability to connect to oracular sources.

Treasures

Catkins

Alder is the only broad leaved tree to put on cones and catkins that remain on the branches in springtime thus making identification easy.

Comfrey ~ protection through healing

Symphytum officinale. Boraginaceae (Borage Family)

A water loving plant that is healing to the nerves and tissues, its folk name is "knitbone" as it helps to fuse broken bones together. Comfrey is a symbol of ancestral foundations. "Bones and skeletons symbolize the basis and foundation of things, and they represent our link with the Ancestors too." [2]

Oracular power

Alder is a tree that loves water and watery depths from which prophetic dreams and oracles flow.

---

2   Carr-Gomm, *The Druid Plant Oracle: Working with the Magical Flora of the Druid Tradition*, p. 36.

Goddess Charms

Saule
Amber–weeping Baltic Sun Goddess who glides through the heavens in Her solar chariot bestowing well-being, health, and fertility onto those below. She spins the sunbeams; Her emblems are the wheel and the rosette. Saule, Goddess of the Sunbeam, the brightness of the sun, shines so brightly only a spinning shield can be seen as She passes in the heavens.

Willow
Saille (sal-yuh)

Salix alba
Salicaceae (Willow Family)

Botanical Highlights

The White willow can grow to a height of 70-80 feet although identifying willows is very difficult due to the way the tree forms. Willows are fairly large trees that are found beside water; they are some of the earliest to flower in the spring. Willow bark is so rich in salicin that it is used as a natural pain reliever.

Tree Essence

White Willow
Salix alba
Green Man Essences ~ " '*True self*' The perception of the self is put in the context of its universal existence. This clarity brings a truer balance within oneself. Ego is cleansed and filled with a sense of bliss and love welling up."

Pussy Willow
Salix discolor
Sweetwater Sanctuary ~ "Helps one stay flexible, personally and planetarily, during major transition times. Allows for growth regardless of seeming obstacles. Helps one think outside the box expanding beyond limiting perceptions."

The Indo-European root of willow is *weik* and from this word we get the word "wicker."

Word Ogham

Morainn mac Moín ~ *"hue of the lifeless"*

Hue of the lifeless
The white undersides of willow leaves are a very pale color giving the tree a "lifeless hue" when the wind blows. The willow is a tree of the moon, known as a tree of enchantment, the poet's tree. Poetic inspiration, prophesy and prophetic dreams spring from the willow's embrace.

Treasures

Basket weaving
Willow's flexible branches are used in wicker work, basket weaving, and to bind birch twigs when making a traditional besom (broom). Willow strips can be woven to make baskets that hold water and willow wicker is used to make funeral caskets.

Mugwort ~ prophesy
Artemisia vulgaris. Asteraceae (Aster Family)
Named for the Moon Goddess Artemis, mugwort is used in works of prophesy and clairvoyance. Taken as a tea, a flower essence for prophetic dreams, or burned as incense, mugwort has many uses including being added to a traditional Japanese food called mochi.

Sally tree, ancestral messages, cycles
"In the ogham alphabet, the willow is *Saille* which became anglicized to 'sally' which means a sudden outburst of emotions, action or expression (to sally forth). The Old French *saille* also means to rush out suddenly and the Latin *salire* means to leap." [3] Willow's energy flows or rushes forth, streaming into consciousness, connecting us with ancestors in a cyclical manner.

---

3 Kindred, *The Power of the Willow Tree*, Imbolc 1997, The White Dragon Magazine. Accessed 18 June 2010 http://www.whitedragon.org.uk/articles/willow.htm

Goddess Charms

Helice
Helice is Goddess of the Willow Stream, a thick stand of willow trees growing along a bank. Helice the Willow-Maid helps us to remember dreams. She gathers them in wicker baskets dripping with moonbeams.

Hawthorn
Huath (hoo-ah)

Crataegus spp.
Rosaceae (Rose Family)

Botanical Highlights

Hawthorns are large shrubs that can grow to the size of small trees. Another name for the hawthorn is Thornapple; their spikey thorn branches make a shelter for birds and other animals. They bear small, reddish, apple-like fruits that offer support to the cardiovascular system. A member of the rose family, they are closely related to rowan, the mountain ash.

Tree Essence

Washington Hawthorn
Crataegus phaenopyrum
Delta Gardens ~ "For releasing unconscious, self-directed anger; developing equanimity and selfless love."

Oneseed Hawthorn, Common or English Hawthorn
 Crataegus monogyna
Green Man Essences ~ " 'Love' Stimulates the healing power of love. Trust. Forgiveness. Helps to cleanse the heart of negativity."

Hawthorn
Crataegus spp.
Sweetwater Sanctuary ~ "Helps elevate the heart to its rightful place, sitting on the throne, where it rules the house of one's being in a harmonious way. For those who are overly engaged in mental processes."

Hawthorn
Crataegus spp.
Woodland Essence ~ "For protection of the heart. For those situations one finds disorienting, uncomfortable or when one needs to deal with those of opposing mind, thought or action."

The origin of the word hawthorn derives from the Anglo-Saxon *"haegthorn,"* which means hedge-thorn.

Word Ogham

Morainn mac Moín ~ *"pack of wolves"*
O'Dubhain ~ *"facing of fears"*

Pack of wolves, facing of fears
Thorn represents an impasse, an obstacle that will be painfully difficult to overcome. It is unavoidable, like a pack of wolves that are about to rip and tear at the flesh. Hawthorn can aid us in overcoming obstacles as we face our fear.

Treasures

Cloutie tree ~ giving thanks
A cloutie (clow-tee) is a bit of fabric, a "rag" that is tied to a tree branch, representing a prayer or a wish.

Cauldron
The cauldron, a symbol for hawthorn is a container that holds water or essence used for cleansing our inner and outer temple.

Fairy tree, wishing well
Fairy trees are said to grow above wells that have healing or curative powers. Hawthorn is one of the four fairy trees guarding the passage to the Otherworld. Clouties are hung to access healing power and to give prayer and thanks to the tree spirits.

Glamours

Fairy glamour and glamoury refer to illusions both seen and created by Otherworld spirits and spell casters.

Hag

Thorn trees are the badge of the crone Goddess known by many names. Hers is the power of the thorn; its healing qualities as well as the dark powers of sorcery. The thorn can open a deep emotional wound, or an old wound, so that healing can take place. It can also be a "thorn in your side" causing pain and festering infection.

Meadowsweet ~ cleansing

Filipendula ulmaria. Rosaceae (Rose Family)

Traditionally the hawthorn Goddess is "made of flowers;" the meadowsweet, oak and broom comprise the Goddess known as "flower" face. The meadowsweet is a hawthorn remedy with pain relieving salicins.

Misfortunes

According to folklore it is ill fortune to bring hawthorn into a house, and at only specific times of the year is it considered acceptable. Hawthorn, known as the tree of misfortunes, can bring a fortunate energy by removing obstacles.

Thorn

Thorn briars and sleeping princesses abound in popular fairy tales. It is said that if you prick your finger upon a thorn you will sleep for a hundred years, entering the fairy realm from which you may never return.

Goddess Charms

The Fairy Goddess Aine

Credited with giving the meadowsweet its scent, She can be called to help you keep your promises. Aine the Fairy Goddess skips through the forest gathering meadowsweet. She pauses at the Hawthorn to hang a cloutie upon the tree then disappears beneath its roots seeking refreshment from a magical wishing well.

Oak
Duir (doo-r)

Quercus robur
Fagaceae (Beech Family)

Botanical Highlights
The oak is long lived with a life span well over 700 years; it is one of the largest trees. Oak leaves can stay on the tree throughout the winter. The bark yields a high amount of tannin, a powerful astringent.

Tree Essence

Red oak
Quercus rubra
Delta Gardens ~ "Helps one experience the 'totality of one's being;' good for those who feel narrow or fearful of exploring new talents, horizons or aspects of the self; a good complement to many expansive therapies."

Common Oak
Quercus robur
Green Man Essences ~ " '*Manifestation*' Absorption and integration of very deep, hidden energy underlying this reality. The desire for stability whilst experiencing the polarities of existence. Ability to manifest one's goals. Channeling energy."

The English word for tree comes from the Indo European word *derwo* (oak).

Word Ogham

Mac ind Óc ~ "*carpenter's work*"
O'Dubhain ~ "*strong and stately*"

Strong and stately, carpenter's work
Strong and stately, the oak commands authority; the wood feels heavier than other woods and is a carpenter's favorite. As the threshold of the year, the oak

month is when the sun reaches its zenith in the sky and plant growth is at it fullest.

Treasures

Acorn
A symbol of patience, luck and protection, acorn is an important food for animals. The word acorn comes from the Old English *aecern*, meaning berry or fruit.

Door of the year, guardian, invisibility
Oak is a door: a doorway to mystical realms, a stout guardian of the inner realm within us. Once we pass through the oak doorway, invisibility is possible and we are able to see what otherwise cannot be seen.

Mistletoe ~ luck & healing
Viscum album. Loranthaceae (Mistletoe Family)
Mistletoe is a sacred Druid plant that grows above the ground on oak or apple trees. Representing great mystery and healing, mistletoe is known as "All heal."

Sacred grove, Sacred flame
In Irish, Kil Dara, means church or temple of the oak, a shrine dedicated to Brighid, Goddess of the Sacred Flame. Today the County Kildare is named for Her sacred grove.

Goddess Charms

Cardea
Roman Goddess of thresholds especially doorways, the time of the Oak marks the hinge of the year at the summer solstice. Cardea guards the threshold of the year in a Sacred Grove of oak. She points to a doorway and offers us an acorn, a symbol of spiritual growth and good luck.

Holly
Tinne (chin-yuh)

Ilex aquifolium
Aquifoliaceae (Holly Family)

Botanical Highlights

Some hollies are deciduous although most are evergreen and shaped into decorative hedgerows. They can withstand the most severe winters and can grow in any kind of soil. The four- petal flowers can bloom randomly at any time of the year, although they most commonly bloom between May and August.

Tree Essence

Holly
Ilex aquifolium
Green Man Essences ~ " *'Power of peace'* Agitated states, balance of mind. Loss of control, panic, lack of self-worth, unhappiness, loneliness. Active expression of love. Non-aggression, peace-loving yet assertive."

The Irish word for holly is *cuilieann* (KWIL-in).

Word Ogham

Morainn mac Moín ~ *"a third part of a wheel, the axle of a wheel"*
Con Culainn ~ *"fires of iron, of a molten iron ingot; a third part of a weapon, made of iron"*
Mac ind Óc ~ *"fires of coal; marrow of charcoal"*

A third part of a wheel, the axle of a wheel, spear
Holly was once one of the three timbers used to make the chariot wheel shaft. The wood of the holly was fashioned to make spear shafts and the holly spear and magical holly dart are a favorite in folk and fairy tales.

Fire, fires of coal; marrow of charcoal
Tinne, the magical name of holly means fire. Holly's wood makes a hot fire which is needed to fashion spears and weapons of war from melted iron. Holly was once used to make charcoal.

Treasures

Holly bears the crown
Symbolic of the waning force of the sun, the holly crown is worn to indicate the holly's victory over the dark time of the year by remaining bright green and vibrant.

Ingot
A smelted bar of iron is called an ingot. An iron ingot, a common crafting material for warrior armor is the charm symbol for holly. *Tinne* the name for holly means "ingot," or "a bar of metal."

Starling
Starlings fly with the strategic precision of an army, pivoting to the left and the right. They are an animal totem for the holly's fighting spirit.

Woad ~ warrior paint
Isatis tinctoria, or German Indigo. Brassicaceae (Mustard Family)
It was believed that warriors went to battle with blue woad painted on their bodies; it is a styptic for wounds and indicates a warrior spirit.

Goddess Charms

Boudica
Iceni Warrior Queen, Boudica led her people to victory annihilating a large Roman legion. Boudica charges through the forest in a chariot with wooden wheels made of holly. She points Her spear upwards toward the future where the might of Her creative force, her fighting spirit overcomes all obstacles.

Hazel

Coll (cull)

Corylus avellana
Corylaceae *(Birch Family)*

Botanical Highlights

Hazel can blossom as early as January although they can leaf relatively late. They usually grow to the size of a large shrub or a small tree. Their leaves open early in the spring and they stay on the branches late into the early winter. The hazelnuts ripen in the fall and can be eaten right from the tree.

Tree Essence

Hazel
Corylus avellana
Green Man Essences ~ " *'Skills'* The flowering of skills. Ability to receive and communicate wisdom. Helps all forms of study. Clears away unwanted debris. Brings more stability and focus in order to integrate useful information."

The word *Corylus* is derived from a Greek word "horys" which means helmet. The hazel is known as "the helmeted one."

Word Ogham

Morainn mac Moín ~ *"fairest of trees"*

Fairest of trees
Hazel is the ultimate symbol of wisdom and divination representing inspired consciousness and our ability to use words to shape reality.

Treasures

Forked twig, finding out things, divination
Diving rods can be made of hazel due to its affinity for water. Hazel has a way of finding hidden things, divining to find water or treasures and performing divination to reveal secrets.

Red Clover ~ wisdom
Trifolium pretense. Fabaceae (Pea Family)
A symbol of good luck and health especially when four-leaved, the clover, a symbol of wisdom is said to spring up in the footprints of the Goddess. The shamrock, a 3-leaf-clover with heart-shaped leaves, is a popular symbol to ward off evil. The three leaves symbolize Goddess in Her three forms of maiden, mother, and crone.

Wisdom, hazelnuts
The hazel is one of the most revered trees in the Druid world because of its connection to wisdom and the Well of Wisdom. Myth tells us that nine hazel trees encircle the Well of Wisdom where the Sacred Salmon swim. In the Druid world, the salmon totem represents the quest for knowledge. The salmon eat hazelnuts that fall into the well thus gaining spots for each nut eaten, their spots representing wisdom gained. Eating hazelnuts is symbolically representative of partaking of the wisdom of the hazel tree.

Goddess Charms

Minerva
Minerva is the Roman Goddess of Wisdom, medicine, the arts, crafts and numbers. Minerva is often seen holding a forked twig symbolic of hidden mysteries. She offers us a hazelnut, the shell of which falls away revealing the sweetest mystery that comes from a personal quest for truth, knowledge and wisdom.

Vine/Blackberry,Mulberry

Muin (muhn)

Vitis vinifera
Vitaceae (Vine Family)

Rubus fructicosus
Rosaceae (Rose Family)

Rubus ursinus
Rosaceae (Rose Family)

Botanical Highlights

Brambles are shrubby briars with astringent roots and edible berries including blackberry, mulberry and raspberry. Blossoms as well as ripe and green fruit are seen on the bush at the same time, an unusual feature for a plant.
Early colonists considered wild North American grapes unsuitable for wine so purple grapes were domesticated in Turkey. The first Old World *Vitis vinifera* wine grapes were cultivated in California at Spanish monasteries.

Tree Essence

Blackberry
Rubus ursinus
FES ~ Decisiveness, directed will.

Mulberry
Morus nigra
Green Man Essences ~ " 'wrath' Powerful emotions released constructively. Freedom from remorse and past pain.   For those hurt by the world and who react with anger and cynicism."

Vine
Vitis vinifera
Healing Herbs ~ Liberation

The bramble is a prickly shrub of the *Rubus* genus, derived from the Old English word "brom" which means broom.

Word Ogham

Morainn mac Moín ~ *"strongest of effort"*
Con Culainn ~ *"pathway of the voice"*

Strongest of effort
The vine spirals upward as it grows appearing to be in a strained position as it attaches to neighboring plants and trees. Tenacious rooted-ness is the way of the bramble.

Pathway of the voice, incantation, trickery
A reference to singing, incantation or, metaphorically, "finding one's voice," speaking truth or trickery, satire, receiving divine messages and interpreting them, all belong to vine.

Treasures

Bramble ~ inspiration
Rubus fructicosus. Rosaceae (Rose Family)
The fruit of the bramble, blackberry, or mulberry makes an intoxicating brew that elevates the spirit and enables contact with spirits through divine inebriation.

Spiral
An ancient symbol connected with both birth and death, the spiral represents the womb of the Earth Goddess. The poet divinely inspired sets out upon a spiritual journey that spirals to immortality.

Trust, ties & binding
Vine indicates emotional ties between people just as it physically binds neighboring plants and trees.

Goddess Charms

The Muses
Muses are nine Goddesses who inspire creativity in artists, poets, and musicians. They bring divine inspiration from the fruit of the bramble, releasing prophetic

powers within us. They sing sweet songs with divine messages that spiral up a hill of poetry to immortality.

Ivy
Gort (gor-it)

Hedera helix
Araliaceae (Ginseng Family)

Botanical Highlights

Ivy is an evergreen climber with small yellow-green flowers that have little or no scent and bloom late in October. The berries ripen the following spring and provide food for birds during hard winters.

Tree Essence

Common Ivy
Hedera helix
Green Man Essences ~ " *'Fear'* Eases hidden fears and anxieties.
Helps to release true feelings and identify needs."

The word Ivy is derived from the Old English *ifig* meaning climber.

Word Ogham

Morainn mac Moín ~ *"sweeter than grasses"*
O'Dubhain ~ *"house of learning"*

Sweeter than grasses, cultivation, hunger
A pasture for animals, a flourishing garden, and a sweet sanctuary of sheltered growth, the ivy represents cultivation and reminds us of the hunger for knowledge and the hunger experienced due to scarcity in unfavorable situations.

House of learning, hunger

Old schools, academies and churches covered with a garment of ivy are places of learning that indicate knowledge found. Hunger for knowledge is quenched in places of learning.

Treasures

Ivy ~ self knowledge

Hedera helix. Araliaceae (Ginseng Family)

A climbing evergreen that represents survival instinct and tenacity, ivy takes us on the journey for self. *Edeand* is the Old Irish word for ivy, meaning that which clothes or covers.

Labyrinth

The labyrinth is a symbol for ivy, representing the quest for inner knowledge and going within oneself.

Poet's crown

A wreath made of entwining ivy is traditionally worn by Irish poets as a symbol of knowledge and inspiration.

Spiral

The spiral itself is named helix as the Latin name for ivy, *Hedera helix*. Helix translates as twinning which refers to the spiraling leaf attachment on the stem.

Spiritual retreat, restoration

Ivy brings the image of a sanctuary, a garden a place where one can retreat to connect with nature and restore our authentic self.

Goddess Charms

The Ivy Goddess Bendis

Great Goddess of Thrace and Lemnos, Fierce Huntress of the Two Spears, Goddess of Forests, Her name means "to tie." Bendis binds the worlds above, between and below. She holds two spears, one pointing up toward the heavens, the other pointing downward to the earth. A poet's crown upon our head, She welcomes us to Her labyrinth where we follow a spiraling path to inner enlightenment.

Reed/Broom
Ngetal (nyeh-tl)

Reed
Phragmites australis. Poaceae or Gramineae (Grass Family)

Broom
Genista scoparius, Cytisus scoparius. Fabaceae (Pea *Family*)

Botanical Highlights

The genus name of the Common Reed *Phragmites* is derived from the Greek meaning "growing in hedges." As with most other grasses, the vertical stems of the Reed live only for a single year, and are replaced with new green shoots in the spring.
Broom is a shrub that is native to England and abundant on sandy pastures and heaths. The Spanish Broom is known as *Genista.* The medicinal use of the astringent branches of the broom known as *Genista* is mentioned in the earliest printed herbals. It had a place in the Pharmacopceia of 1618; there is a great amount of tannin in the bark.

Tree Essence

 Scotch Broom
Cytisus scoparius
FES ~ Optimism

The word reed comes from the root *canna* meaning law, a canon, a cane or walking cane.

Word Ogham

Morainn mac Moín ~ *"a physician's strength; broom"*
Mac ind Óc ~ *"robe of physicians"*
O'Dubhain ~ *"pathway to life'*

Robe of physician's, a physician's strength
The metaphorical physician's robe gives the impression of protection as does the reed which shelters birds and delicate plant life; this sheltering is the strength of the physician who serves those who seek improved health.

Pathway to life
Ó Dubhain describes the reed as " 'bending and flowing with the winds.' The reed, in effect, 'bows its head' to the storms and allows them to pass. Its strength is its ability to yield." [4]

Treasures

Broom
Cytisus scoparius. Fabaceae (Pea Family)
Shelters birds as well as other plants; the wood is gathered to make a traditional broom used for sweeping away unwanted energies.

Medicinal plants
Reed/broom is a sign of healing for both the healer and the wound to be healed; it also indicates the charm, incantation or prayer that is spoken or sung to enable the healing process.

Plantain ~ wound dressing
Plantago major. Plantaginaceae (Plantain Family)
Children can be taught to chew and apply this healing plant for small scrapes & cuts.

Preservation, knowledge, memory, pen
Traditionally reed was used to thatch roofs and make pens; this refers to preservation, the preservation of the family's home as well as preservation of knowledge and memory.

Teasel ~ promotes energy
Dipsacus sylvestris. Dipsacaceae (Teasel Family)
The flower essence rebalances energy levels and remedies energy loss.

---

4   Ó Dubhain, Ogham Divination Part VIII, p. 7.

Goddess Charms

The Goddess Cerridwen

Cerridwen is the Keeper of the Cauldron of Inspiration, wisdom, memory and great healing. She sings incantations over Her healing cauldron where the medicinal properties of herbs become an elixer for your health. She sings a charm over the wounded parts of ourselves and offers us a taste from Her chalice containing a healing infusion.

Elder

Ruis (rweesh)

Sambucus nigra
Adoxaceae (Muskroot Family)

Botanical Highlights

A small tree rarely growing more than 30 feet, it produces stems from its base and replaces dead wood with new shoots. Elder roots easily from cut branches planted directly into the ground. Its hollow branches are filled with pith and covered with spots through which the elder breathes. Elder berries can be made into medicinal syrup that is beneficial for the entire family; birds love them too.

Tree Essence

 Black Elder
Sambucus nigra
Green Man Essences ~ " *'Self worth'* Calms aggression, brings stability, love and forgiveness. Balances self-image. For times of transformation and change. Good for fretful children."

American Elder
Sambucus canadensis
Woodland Essence ~ "Holds the joy and exuberance, the magic and mystery of the plant spirits. Offers protection on the etheric and spiritual planes."

The name elder comes from the Anglo Saxon root *aeld* meaning fire.

Word Ogham

Morainn mac Moín ~ *"intensest of blushes"*
Con Culainn ~ *"glow of anger"*
Mac ind Óc ~ *"redness of faces"*

Intensest of blushes, glow of anger, redness of faces, redness
Elder's power and magic is one of intensity like a fiery flame or the red color of an angry face. To "see red" is a metaphor for anger. *Ruad* is the Old Irish word for the red color associated with elder.

Treasures

Healing tree
This tree's berries, flowers, leaves and bark offer healing qualities, although the berries are most popular. Elder is thought to cure just about anything and has been called "the medicine chest of the common people".

Madder ~ redness
Rubia sp. Rubiaceae (Madder Family)
The madder produces a rich red dye indicating a time of transition in a woman's life, a time away.

Rue ~ protection
Ruta graveolens. Rutaceae (Rue Family)
Ruta aids in recuperation, promotes health and provides protection as a flower essence or a sprig hung nearby. Sometimes called "herb of grace," the *cima de ruta* (sprig of rue) is a magical charm.

Goddess Charms

Cailleach (Kye – lyhkh), Mother of the Bones
The Cailleach as the Winter Goddess and the Hag of Winter owns this tree. It is considered unlucky to take some of its wood unless a prayer is said and an offering is made. As Mother of the Bones, Cailleach is the wild, untamable, Goddess of Ecstasy and Death; Her house made of the bones of the dead. In Russian fairy tales, the Mother of the Bones is known as Baba Yaga whose bone

house stands upon chicken feet. In an ecstatic trance, Cailleach offers us a healing medicine chest brimming with elder leaves and berries. Upon the chest is a sprig of rue and magical tree charms that foretell our future.

A sprig of rue

& magical tree charms

Tree Invocation

I stand upon the Sacred Earth
the Ancient Sea surrounds me
Endless Sky above me
I give thanks to You
Great Mother of Healing
Sacred Grove
Spirit Tree
and the Holy
(say the name of your tree)
Blessings
Gratitude
Blessed Be

Tree Months

Birch ~   December 24 ~ January 20
Rowan   ~   January 21 ~ February 17
Ash ~   February 18 ~ March 17
Alder   ~   March 18 ~ April 14
Willow   ~   April 15 ~ May 12
Hawthorn   ~   May 13 ~ June 9
Oak ~   June 10 ~ July 7
Holly ~   July 8 ~ August 4
Hazel ~   August 5 ~ September 1
Vine/Bramble ~   September 2 ~ September 29
Ivy ~   September 30 ~ October 27
Reed/Broom ~   October 28 ~ November 24
Elder ~   November 25 ~ December 23

Tree Seasons

Samhain ~   November Eve ~ Reed
Yule ~   December 21 ~ Elder
Brigantia ~   February Eve ~ Rowan
Ostara ~   March 21 ~ Alder
Beltane ~   May Eve ~ Willow
Litha ~   June 21 ~ Oak
Lammas ~   August Eve ~ Holly
Mabon ~   September 21 ~ Vine

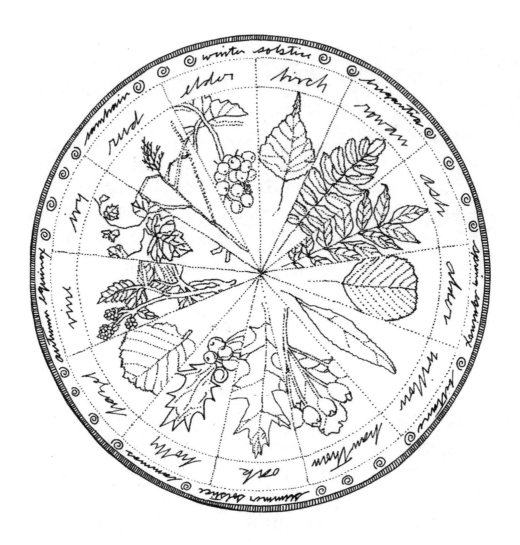

The Celtic Tree Calendar

Guidelines for Tree Essences

Selecting Essences

Taking tree essences is a way of experiencing the trees at a deeper level. You can choose trees that correspond to planets in your natal astrology chart or use intuition and select them by dowsing or kinesiology.

How Essences are used

You can take them directly from the stock bottle. Individual essences you buy from the store are sold as "stock" strength. Follow the suggested dose on the bottle as these will vary, place drops of the essence under your tongue, on wrists, in a glass of water, or make an essence spray. Shake the stock bottle gently a few times before taking drops from the bottle. Avoid touching the dropper to teeth and mouth to prevent transferring bacteria to the bottle.

Mix Them in a Glass of Water

Add drops to a glass of water; stir the water in a clockwise motion to mix in the essence. Sip throughout the day. This mixture can last for 1-3 days; after that prepare a fresh mixture. It doesn't matter what size the water glass is.

How Long to Take Essences

You can use intuition to determine how long to take them, ranging from a day to a month. You could begin taking them on the new moon, ending on the following new moon and journal your experiences throughout the month.

Tree & Flower Essences are safe, natural and non-toxic. They are not intended as a substitute for regular professional medical care.

Tree Affirmation Cards

Make your own using the affirmation included for each tree. Carry them with you throughout the day, repeating the affirmation when you take your essence to cultivate individual tree qualities.

Lady of Wisdom
bring me
good fortune
and knowledge

Tree Tokens

Bark, catkin, twig, bud, and leaf, these are unique to
each tree type; they are the signature of the tree. You
will find these on the forest floor especially after a
heavy rain. Collect them for your tree and
carry a small token with you

Tree Contemplation

Ground and center, take a deep breath,
read the tree poem,
contemplate your tree

Tree Calendar

Use the tree calendar to discover when
you can experience tree energy
throughout the year.

Further Reading

Barret, Leigh Gadell. *The Tree Mothers: Living Wisdom of the Ogham Trees*. Lulu Publishing, 2010.

Laurie, Erynn Rowan. *Ogham: Weaving Word Wisdom*. Stafford, UK, Megalithica Books, 2007.

Quarrie Deanne. *Annym Billagh: Healing with the Tree Ogham*. Austin, Texas: Apple Branch Press, 2009.

- - -. *Dancing with Goddess*. Austin, Texas, : Apple Branch Press, 2009.

- - -. *Ogham Twigs*. Austin, Texas: Apple Branch Press, 2010.

- - -. *From the Branch: The Ogham for Spiritual Growth*. Austin, Texas: Apple Branch Press, 2010.

Supplies

Astrology

Astrodienst (free natal astrology chart) www.astro.com
Paterson, Helena. *The Celtic Moon Sign Kit*. New York: Fireside, Simon & Schuster, 1999.

Tree & Flower Essences
Company catalogues are referenced for essence descriptions.

Delta Gardens, Newburyport, MA (red oak, washington hawthorn, white birch) www.deltagardens.com

FES Flower Essence Society, Nevada City, CA (blackberry, vine)
 www.fesflowers.com/

Green Man Essences, UK www.greenmantrees.demon.co.uk/index.html

Sweetwater Sanctuary Essences, Danby, VT (hawthorn, pussy willow) www.plantspirithealing.com/index.htm

Woodland Essences, Cold Brook, NY (black birch, elder, hawthorn, white ash) www.woodlandessence.com/

Bibliography

Barret, Leigh Gadell. *The Tree Mothers: Living Wisdom of the Ogham Trees.* Lulu Publishing, 2010.

Blamires, Steve. *Celtic Tree Mysteries: Practical Druid Magic & Divination.* St. Paul, MN: Llewellyn Publications, 1997.

Bleakley, Alan. *Fruits of the Moon Tree: The Medicine Wheel & Transpersonal Psychology.* London, UK: Gateway Books, 1984.

Brimble, L.J.F. *Trees in Britain.* London, England: MacMillan and Co. Ltd., 1946.

Carr-Gomm, Philip and Stephanie. *The Druid Plant Oracle: Working with the magical flora of the Druid Tradition.* London: The Connections Book Publishing, 2007.

Dalton, David. *Stars of the Meadow: Exploring Medicinal Herbs as Flower Essences.* Great Barrington, Massachusetts: Lindisfarne Books, 2006.

Ellison, Rev. Robert Lee. *The Secret Language of the Druids.* Tuscon: ADF Publishing, 2007.

Fergus, Charles. *Trees of New England: A Natural History.* Guilford, Connecticut: The Globe Pequot Press, 2005.

Gifford, Jane. *The Celtic Wisdom of Trees: Mysteries, Magic and Medicine.* New York: Sterling Publishing Co., 2000.
Graves, Robert. *The White Goddess.* New York: Farrar, Straus and Giroux, 1948.

Greer, John Michael, *The Druid Magic Handbook: Ritual Magic Rooted in the Living Earth.* San Francisco, CA: Red Wheel/Weiser, LLC, 2007.

Grieve, M. "A Modern Herbal." Volume I and II. 18 June 2010. http://botanical.com/botanical/mgmh/mgmh.html.

Hopman, Ellen Evert . *A Druid's Herbal of Sacred Tree Medicine.* Rochester Vermont: Destiny Books, 2008.

- - -.*A Druid's Herbal for the Sacred Earth Year.* Rochester, Vermont: Destiny Books 1995.

Kerr, Linda. "Folklore and Practical Uses." *Hazel Nut* . *Faerie Faith*. 1993. 18 June 2010. http://www.faeriefaith.net/HazelNut/HazelNut.html.

Kindred, Glennie. "The Power of the Willow Tree." *The White Dragon Magazine* Imbolc 1997. 18 June 2010. http://www.whitedragon.org.uk/articles/willow.htm.

Kynes, Sandra. *Whispers from the Woods*: The Lore and Magic of Trees. Woodbury, Minnesota: Llewellyn Publications, 2006.

Landis, James Clifford. *The Faerie Faith and the Beth-Luis-Nion Celtic Lunar Tree Calendar*. Auburn, Alabama: Auburn University, 2002.

Laurie, Erynn Rowan. *Ogham: Weaving Word Wisdom*. Stafford, UK, Megalithica Books, 2007.

Matthews, John. *The Celtic Shaman's Pack*. Shaftesbury, Dorset: Element Books Limited, 1995.

More, David and White, John. *The Illustrated Encyclopedia of Trees. Second Edition.* Portland: Timber Press, 2005.

Mountforth, Paul Rhys. *Ogham: The Celtic Oracle of the Trees*. Rochester, VT: Destiny Books, 2001.

Murray, Liz and Colin. *The Celtic Tree Oracle; A System of Divination*.New York: St. Martin's Press, 1988.

O'Dubhain, Searles. *Ogham Divination Part VIII*, Keltria Lughnasadh Fall Issue 35 . 1997: 2-8.

- - -. *Ogham Divination Part IX*, Keltria Samhain Winter Issue 36 .1997: 1-8.

- - -. *Ogham Divination Part X*, Keltria Imbolc Spring Issue 37 .1998: 2-7.

- - -. *Ogham Divination Part XI*, Keltria Beltaine Summer Issue 38 .1998: 4-5.

Paterson, Jacqueline Memory. *Tree Wisdom: The Definitive Guidebook*. London: Thorsons, 1966.

Pennick, Nigel and Jackson, Nigel. *The Celtic Oracle: A Complete Guide to Using the Cards.* London: The Aquarian Press 1992.

Pennick, Nigel. *Magical Alphabets*. San Francisco: Red Wheel/Weiser, LLC, 1992.

- - -. *Ogham and Coelbren: Keys to the Celtic Mysteries*. UK: Capall Bann, 2000.

Quarrie Deanne. *Annym Billagh: Healing with the Tree Ogham*. Austin, Texas: Apple Branch Press, 2009.

- - -. *From the Branch: The Ogham for Spiritual Growth*. Austin, Texas: Apple Branch Press, 2010.

- - -. *Ogham Twigs*. Austin, Texas: Apple Branch Press, 2010.

Sibley, David Allen. *The Sibley Guide to Trees*. New York: Alfred A. Knopf, 2009.

Gratitude

To Goddess
& the Trees